BASEBALL SUPERSTARS

2016

By K. C. Kelley

SCHOLASTIC

Photos ©: cover top left: Chris Bernacchi/AP Images; cover top right: Joshua Sarner/Icon Sportswire/Newscom; cover center and throughout: Jamie Roach/Shutterstock, Inc.; cover bottom: Matt Masin/AP Images; back cover background: Prixel Creative/Shutterstock, Inc.; 1 background: winui/Shutterstock, Inc.; 1 left: Joe Sargent/Getty Images; 1 center: Brad Mangin/Getty Images; 1 right: Marcio Jose Sanchez/AP Images; 2-3 background and throughout: Prixel Creative/Shutterstock, Inc.; 2 main and throughout: ChromaCo/Shutterstock, Inc.; 4 top: Charlie Riedel/AP Images; 4 player vector and throughout: Terry Underwood Evans/Shutterstock, Inc.; 5: George Nikitin/AP Images; 6 top: Ric Tapia/AP Images; 7: John Bazemore/AP Images; 8 top: Tony Gutierrez/AP Images; 9: Kathy Willens/AP Images; 10 top: Rick Madonik/Getty Images; 11: Jim McIsaac/Getty Images; 12 top: Rob Tringali/Getty Images; 13: Norm Hall/Getty Images; 14 top: John Raoux/AP Images; 15: Mitchell Layton/Getty Images; 16 top: Jeff Roberson/AP Images; 17: Brad Mangin/Getty Images; 18 top: Charlie Riedel/AP Images; 19: Dustin Bradford/AP Images; 20 top: Ric Tapia/AP Images; 21: Orlin Wagner/AP Images; 22 top: David Goldman/AP Images; 23: Andrew Dieb/AP Images; 24 top: Chris O'Meara/AP Images; 25: Chris Bernacchi/AP Images; 26 top: Fred Vuich/AP Images; 27: Joe Sargent/Getty Images; 28 top: John Cordes/AP Images; 29: Marcio Jose Sanchez/AP Images; 30 top: David Goldman/AP Images; 30 bottom: Pat Sullivan/AP Images; 31 top: Frank Jansky/Icon Sportswire/Newscom; 31 bottom: Tony Dejak/AP Images.

ISBN 978-1-338-03276-5

10 9 8 7 6 5 4 3 2 1   16 17 18 19 20

Printed in the U.S.A. 40
First printing 2016

Book design by Rocco Melillo

CONTENTS

STAT NOTES:

ALL STATS ARE COMPLETE THROUGH THE 2015 MLB SEASON.

W = WINS

ERA = EARNED RUN AVERAGE

IP = INNINGS PITCHED

SO = STRIKEOUTS

AVG = BATTING AVERAGE

HR = HOME RUNS

RBI = RUNS BATTED IN

OPS = ON-BASE PERCENTAGE PLUS SLUGGING PERCENTAGE

NOLAN ARENADO
COLORADO ROCKIES

Position: THIRD BASE

Height: 6'2"
Weight: 205 lbs

Throws: Right
Bats: Right

First MLB Season: 2013

Talk about a breakout season! In 2015, Nolan Arenado had more homers and RBI than in his previous two MLB seasons . . . combined! The Colorado Rockies' slugging All-Star third baseman put on a power display from the first game of the year. Add to that the defensive skill that has earned him three Gold Glove Awards, and you've got one of the game's brightest young stars.

Nolan grew up in Southern California. His father, Fernando, was born in Cuba but moved to the United States when he was six years old. In California, Fernando played baseball before he started a baseball-loving family. (Nolan's younger brother, Jonah, is also a pro and plays in the San Francisco Giants' minor-league system.) How much did Fernando like baseball? He named his oldest son after his favorite player: Hall of Fame pitcher Nolan Ryan.

Nolan Arenado was a slugging star at El Toro High School but was not considered a very good defensive player. Still, the Rockies took him in the second round of the 2009 MLB Draft. Year by year, he moved up the minor-league ladder. He continued his solid hitting but spent most of his time working with coaches on his defense.

Nolan knew that he could not be just a slugger.

In 2013, Nolan became the Rockies' starting third baseman. He became the first National League rookie to win a Gold Glove at third base. In fact, he became only the 10th rookie at any position ever to get the coveted award.

While Nolan's defense was great, his big-league hitting was just okay. He learned a lot from veteran teammates such as All-Star shortstop Troy Tulowitzki. "Tulo" and other vets suggested that Nolan lose some weight. He worked hard in the off-season and entered 2015 more than 20 pounds lighter. That made him quicker and more powerful. His coaches also saw that he was learning at the plate, making his at-bats more focused and assured.

Nolan got off to a hot start, with a homer and 4 RBI on Opening Day. He never let up and was among the league leaders in all three Triple Crown categories (home runs, RBI, and batting average) for most of the first half of the season. His average dropped, but his power continued. His 42 homers tied for the most in the National League, while his 130 RBI led the Majors! He also had 354 total bases, tops among all hitters. It was a dream season that could signal more power in the future!

STAT BOX	AVG	HR	RBI	OPS
2015	.287	42	130	.898
CAREER	.281	70	243	.816

How good was Nolan in high school? He was a first-team All-American and the league MVP. His .517 batting average was a school record. As a result, he became the first player from El Toro High to have his number retired. The second? His teammate Austin Romine, who now plays for the New York Yankees!

NOLAN ARENADO

JAKE ARRIETA

CHICAGO CUBS

Position: PITCHER

Height: 6'4"
Weight: 225 lbs

Throws: Right
Bats: Right

First MLB Season: 2010

For pitcher Jake Arrieta, it was worth the wait. The Chicago Cubs' hard-throwing righty had one of the best pitching seasons ever in 2015. It came, however, after a hard road that included stops in six minor-league cities. Most of his great work in 2015 came, also, after the All-Star break. That's when he put on a show of pitching excellence that led to his winning the Cy Young Award as the National League's best pitcher!

Jake's long road to the top started in Plano, Texas, where he grew up. After a year in junior college, Jake was a star at Texas Christian University. In his first season at TCU, he led the nation with 14 wins. After another solid season as a junior in 2007, he was selected by the Baltimore Orioles in the fifth round of the MLB Draft.

Jake spent three seasons moving through the Orioles' minor-league system. He played on four teams in Arizona, Virginia, and Maryland. He did okay but was not really a star. The Orioles gave him a shot with the big club in 2010, though, and he went 6–6. He won a few more games with them but did not really perform as well as he had hoped.

The Orioles traded Jake to the Cubs in 2013. After more minor-league visits in Iowa, Florida, and Tennessee, Jake returned to the big leagues. What a difference this time around!

Jake had a solid season in 2014, winning 10 games. During the off-season, he increased his workouts and improved his flexibility. (He also worked out by carrying his two young children in a backpack while hiking trails near his Austin, Texas, home.)

The workouts worked . . . plus, it helped that the Cubs were much improved as a team.

In 2015, Jake was 9–5 by midseason, but he didn't earn a selection to the All-Star Game. When the season resumed after the break, however, Jake caught fire. He was 3–1 during the rest of July. Then, from August 4 to the end of the season, he didn't lose once! Jake won 11 consecutive games, with a miniscule ERA of 0.75. That was the best ever for a pitcher over the second half of a season. In six of those games, he did not allow a run. Best of all, Jake's heroics helped the Cubs reach the playoffs for the first time since 2008.

When all the numbers were in, Jake's 22 wins, 33 starts, and 3 shutouts led the NL. His 1.77 ERA was second in the league and the best of his career by far. His ERA was also the lowest by a Cubs' pitcher since all the way back in 1919! He edged out the Dodgers' Zack Greinke for the Cy Young Award.

STAT BOX	W	ERA	IP	SO
2015	22	1.77	229.0	236
CAREER	56	3.70	795.1	717

BEFORE THE BIGS

Jake has worn red, white, and blue for another team: the US National squad. In 2006, he won 4 games when that team captured gold at the World University Games. In the 2008 Olympics, he was the winning pitcher in the United States' victory over China.

JAKE ARRIETA

XANDER BOGAERTS

BOSTON RED SOX

Position: SHORTSTOP/THIRD BASE

Height: 6'1"
Weight: 210 lbs

Throws: Right
Bats: Right

First MLB Season: 2013

Boston's star infielder is a future superstar . . . and he can tell you that in four languages! Xander Bogaerts (he pronounces his name "ZAN-der BO-garts") grew up on the Caribbean island of Aruba. That island is actually part of the Netherlands, so Xander learned Dutch as a child. The other official language of Aruba is called Papiamento. Xander also learned English and Spanish while growing up in and around baseball. In any language, he's a great player.

Xander's uncle first helped Xander and his twin brother, Jair, learn baseball basics. Xander started out by hitting almonds pitched to him by his uncle. Imagine how big a baseball looked to him after hitting tiny almonds! By the time Xander was nine, he was good enough at hitting baseballs to join a traveling all-star Little League team.

Other players from his island home had made it to the big leagues. From the neighboring island of Curaçao came outfielder Andruw Jones, who played 17 years with the Atlanta Braves and other teams, and Sidney Ponson, who pitched in 12 big-league seasons. Xander hoped to join their ranks.

In 2009, when he was only 16, he was signed to a pro contract by the Red Sox. Xander played in a Dominican Republic summer league for a Red Sox farm club, then moved to the United States in 2011. He next played in Greenville, South Carolina, where he had 16 homers in just 72 games. He was showing a rare combination of fielding skill and power at the plate. By 2013, he was named the Minor League Player of the Year and had gotten his first taste of the big leagues. And what a taste: Xander joined Boston in time to be the starting shortstop as the Red Sox won the World Series in 6 games over the Cardinals!

Xander put it all together in 2015. He combined clutch hitting with a great batting eye, and he played solid defense as the team's starting shortstop. His 81 RBI were a career high, and he led the American League with 151 singles. Put it all together, and his .320 batting average placed him second in the league. He won the Silver Slugger Award as the league's top-hitting shortstop.

Xander is one of several young islanders making a mark in the Majors. Didi Gregorius of the New York Yankees and Kenley Jansen of the Los Angeles Dodgers, for instance, also were raised in the islands. Now the young players on Aruba and Curaçao are looking up to Xander as a role model. They picked a good one!

STAT BOX	AVG	HR	RBI	OPS
2015	.320	7	81	.776
Career	.291	23		.730

BEFORE THE BIGS

Xander not only got to play a lot of Little League baseball, but he also got to travel. His teams from Aruba went to other Caribbean islands to play in tournaments. He later gained more international experience when he played for the Netherlands in the 2011 World Cup and the 2013 World Baseball Classic.

XANDER BOGAERTS

JOSH DONALDSON

TORONTO BLUE JAYS

Position: THIRD BASE

Height: 6'0"
Weight: 220 lbs

Throws: Right
Bats: Right

First MLB Season: 2010

Baseball fans and experts could see it coming. They watched Josh Donaldson smash baseballs all over the place, and they knew: Someday, this guy was going to dominate. It finally fell into place in 2015 as Josh played in . . . a new place. Sometimes, there is nothing better than a change of scenery to get things flowing. In his first season with the Toronto Blue Jays, Josh led the American League in runs and RBI. He was the clear winner of the AL MVP award.

Josh grew up in Florida and Alabama. He faced tough times when he was a youngster. His father was put in prison after committing several crimes. On the baseball field, Josh found a way to work out his emotions. Poor baseballs!

In high school, Josh was a star in several sports, including football. Baseball was his best, though, and he set many school records. He then played three seasons at Auburn University, where he switched to catcher for a while. The Chicago Cubs chose him in the 2007 MLB Draft but traded him to the Oakland Athletics in 2009. He played briefly with the A's in 2010, then became a full-time third baseman in the minor leagues. He had solid seasons with the Sacramento River Cats, with his eye on the big leagues.

By 2013, he had settled in as the starting third baseman for Oakland. Though the A's home in the Coliseum is not hitter friendly, Josh didn't mind. He slugged 24 homers and drove in 93 runs. His 2014 season was even better, with 29 homers and 98 RBI. He also was named to his first All-Star team that year. In both seasons, Josh finished in the top 10 in voting for AL MVP. It looked like Oakland was all set at third base for years to come.

But in a surprising off-season move, Oakland traded its big star to Toronto. The Blue Jays sent four players to the A's to get their man. In his new home, Josh had his best season, crushing 41 homers and knocking in an AL-best 123 runs. He also scored 122 runs and was named the AL Player of the Month for September. Josh's season-ending power helped the Blue Jays make the playoffs for the first time since 1993. In the playoffs, Josh had 3 homers and 8 RBI, but the Blue Jays lost the AL Championship Series to the Royals.

Josh will need a bigger den for all the hardware he brought home in 2015. Along with the MVP trophy, he earned the Hank Aaron Award as the AL's top offensive player. He was named the Major League Player of the Year by *Sporting News*. And, not surprisingly, he won the AL Silver Slugger Award for third basemen. Everyone saw it coming—it just took a while!

STAT BOX

	AVG	HR	RBI	OPS
2015	.297	41	123	.939
CAREER	.276	104	351	.844

BEFORE THE BIGS

When he was a kid, Josh loved to collect baseball cards. He would save his money and go to the store to choose favorites. One he particularly loved was Atlanta Braves outfielder Ron Gant. Even today, Josh can't wait to get the new boxes of cards when they come out each spring.

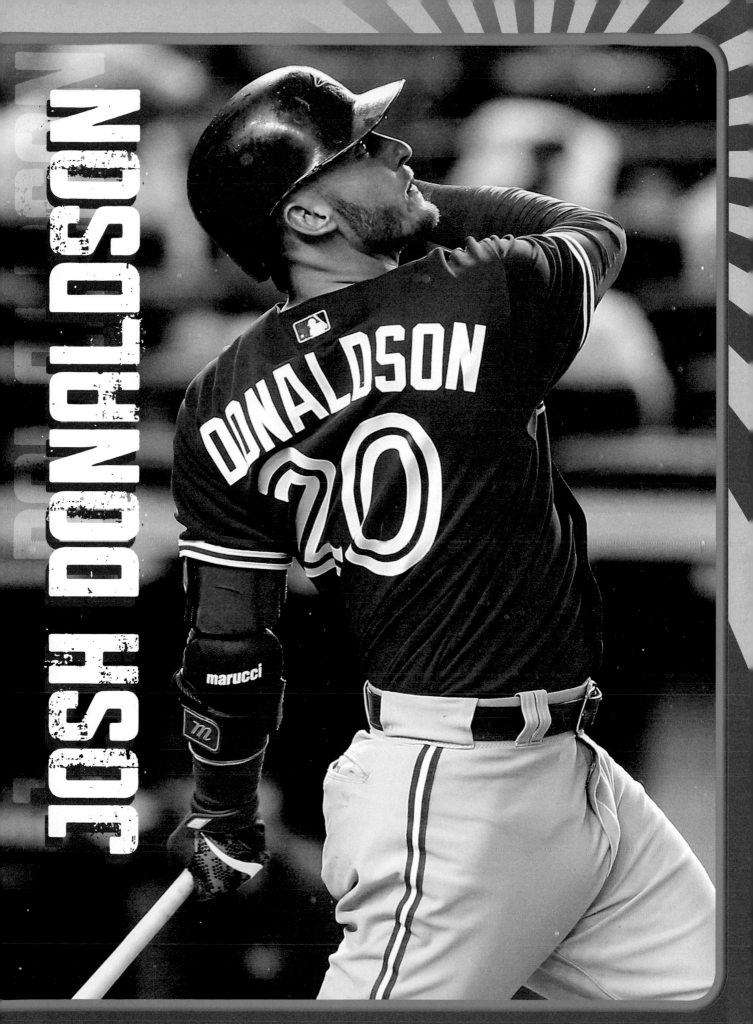

JOSH DONALDSON

PAUL GOLDSCHMIDT

ARIZONA DIAMONDBACKS

Position: FIRST BASE

Height: 6'3"
Weight: 225 lbs

Throws: Right
Bats: Right

First MLB Season: 2011

For most of the past four seasons, this big first baseman has been one of the best all-around hitters in the game. An RBI machine, Paul Goldschmidt has tons of power, but he can also hit for a high average. That's a rare combination these days, and the Arizona Diamondbacks are glad he's doing it all for them!

Paul grew up near Houston, Texas, and baseball was his sport. When he reached high school, however, he grew quite a bit. The football team wanted him to join, but he loved baseball too much. As a senior, he helped his school win the state championship, which he remembers as one of his greatest moments.

Paul chose to play in college at Texas State University in San Marcos. His power hitting made him a star. By the time he left Texas State after three seasons, he was the school's all-time leader in home runs, doubles, and many other batting stats. The Diamondbacks drafted Paul in the eighth round in 2009.

In two of his three minor-league seasons, Paul was named the league MVP—in the California League and in the Southern League. As usual, his home-run hitting was his biggest weapon. With 83 homers, he had done all the damage he could in the minors. By the summer of 2011, it was time to head to Arizona.

Paul got off to a good start in the big leagues: He had a hit in his first at-bat. In his second game, he hit his first home run. He finished with 8 home runs in only 48 games played. He got some postseason experience, too, helping the D-Backs reach the National League Division Series. In 2012, he was a full-time starter at first base and improved in every area of hitting.

In 2013, Paul had his best season, leading the NL with 36 homers and 125 RBI. He also led the league with a .952 OPS, an important stat that combines power and getting on base. That year, he hit .302, the first of three consecutive seasons above .300. He also showed his all-around skills, winning the Gold Glove Award for fielding excellence. In 2014, a broken hand kept him out of more than 50 games. Still, he knocked in 69 runs and made his second All-Star team.

By 2015, it was no secret that Paul was one of the game's best hitters. He was among the league leaders in several hitting categories. His total of 110 RBI was second in the NL, while his .321 average and 323 total bases each ranked third in the league. He also won his second Gold Glove Award.

Good thing he decided to stick to baseball!

STAT BOX	AVG	HR	RBI	OPS
2015	.321	33	110	1.005
CAREER	.299	176	482	.950

BEFORE THE BIGS

Paul not only spent lots of time on the baseball field in high school, he also had a part-time job working at the local batting cages!

PAUL GOLDSCHMIDT

BRYCE HARPER

WASHINGTON NATIONALS

Position: OUTFIELD

Height: 6'3"
Weight: 215 lbs

Throws: Right
Bats: Left

First MLB Season: 2012

Expectations can be hard to live up to. When Bryce Harper was 16, he was on the cover of *Sports Illustrated*. The magazine called him the "Chosen One." Some young people can't handle that attention. Sometimes, they don't live up to the hype. In Bryce's case, however, he has gone even further than those high hopes. Along with Mike Trout of the Los Angeles Angels, Bryce is at the top of the list of "best players in the game." In 2015, the Washington Nationals star had the best season so far of his remarkable career, when he earned his first National League MVP award. Here's guessing it won't be his last.

Bryce grew up in Las Vegas, Nevada, and quickly showed that baseball was his future. When he was just three years old, he took part in a T-ball league for six-year-olds! He was playing on traveling all-star teams by the time he was 10. As a high school sophomore catcher, he hit .626 and made the *SI* cover. He told a reporter for the magazine that his goals were simple: "Make the Hall of Fame. Be considered the greatest baseball player who ever lived." Even Bryce had great expectations.

In order to start playing pro as soon as he could, Bryce earned his high-school equivalency degree after only two years. At 17, he played one season of junior-college baseball at Southern Nevada. All he did was set several school records, hit .443, and lead the team to the Junior College World Series. Oh, yes, he also was named the nation's top college player, a rare honor for a J.C. player. In June 2010, the Nationals made him the first overall pick of the MLB Draft.

As great as Bryce was, he still needed a bit of time in the minor leagues. He quickly moved up the ranks, making the Nationals' Triple-A team in April 2012. Then it was time. The 19-year-old outfielder was brought up to the Nationals for good later that month. Or should that be "for great"?

Bryce hit 22 homers, made his first All-Star Game, and was named the 2012 NL Rookie of the Year. In 2013, he again played well but was not quite living up to what he expected. He had become a very good big-league outfielder, but "very good" was not good enough. Bryce had the attitude that he must be the best . . . nothing less. His hard-charging style hurt him in 2014, when he missed more than 60 games with a hand injury. He suffered it when diving hard into third base on a slide.

After the injury, some wondered if the wonder boy could live up to the hype. In 2015, he proved that he could. The 22-year-old had one of the best offensive seasons ever for a player his age. He tied for the league lead with 42 homers and topped all NL players with 118 runs scored. He was a unanimous choice as MVP and now is one of the most feared hitters in the league. From cover star to superstar . . . who knows what's next?

STAT BOX	AVG	HR	RBI	OPS
2015	.330	42	99	1.109
CAREER	.283	97	248	.908

In high school, Bryce played on an all-star team that also included a hard-hitting infielder named Kris Bryant. A few years later, the two each earned major awards in 2015. Bryce was the NL MVP, while Kris was the NL Rookie of the Year with the Chicago Cubs. That's a pretty tough travel team!

MATT HARVEY

NEW YORK METS

Position: PITCHER

Height: 6'4"	**Throws:** Right
Weight: 215 lbs	**Bats:** Right

First MLB Season: 2012

Matt Harvey is known as one of the toughest pitchers in baseball. Batters fear his fastball. They know he will battle to get them out with every pitch. But Matt is just as tough off the field. After bursting onto the scene with great seasons for the New York Mets in 2012 and 2013, he had to miss an entire year with an arm injury. The story of his road back to the top—and to the World Series—makes him more than just an All-Star.

Matt grew up in Connecticut, where he had a coach right at home. His father, Ed, was a high school coach for many years. When Matt was old enough, he joined his father's team. Together, they won three state titles. Matt, of course, was in the thick of it as the team's star pitcher. Even then, his fastball was legendary, and he was named an All-American. One magazine called him the top prospect in the nation! With his family, he also often attended Mets and Yankees games in nearby New York City.

The Los Angeles Angels drafted Matt out of high school, but he chose to play at the University of North Carolina. With the Tar Heels, he was 22–7 in three seasons, striking out 263 batters.

In 2010, he was the seventh overall pick in the draft . . . by the Mets!

After two seasons in the minors, Matt was brought up to the big leagues in 2012. He got off to a fantastic start, striking out 11 batters in five innings in his first game. However, he struggled later in 2012 and ended up winning only 3 games. It was more off-season workouts for Matt, who burned to be the best.

In 2013, he had a rocket start. He began the season with 8 wins in his first 10 games. By midseason, he was the clear choice as the starter for the National League team in the All-Star Game. It was played at Citi Field, Matt's and the Mets' home park. He was doing great, with a 2.27 ERA and 191 strikeouts in only 178 innings. But in August, he felt a pop in his arm. He had damaged a key part of his elbow. Doctors told him that he needed surgery to repair the arm. He would not be able to pitch the rest of 2013 or in 2014.

Matt went from being a superstar and the hero of New York City to the invisibility of the workout room. He attacked his exercises like he went after hitters—100 percent hard! By the start of 2015, Matt was ready to take the mound.

He quickly showed that he was his old self, winning a career-best 13 games. By the end of the season, he had once again become the ace of a great Mets staff. In fact, he helped New York reach the World Series for the first time since 2000! Matt was crushed when the team lost to the Royals. But the experience made him want to work even harder to bring a championship to New York.

STAT BOX

2015	13	2.71	189.1	188
CAREER	25	2.53	427.0	449

When Matt was in fourth grade, his teacher gave out baseball cards to students who did well. Matt got a card showing a star pitcher. He told his teacher, "I'm going to be better than him." Turns out Matt was right!

FELIX HERNANDEZ

SEATTLE MARINERS

Position: PITCHER

Height: 6'3"
Weight: 225 lbs

Throws: Right
Bats: Right

First MLB Season: 2005

Talk about fast starts! When Felix Hernandez was just 14 years old, he could throw a baseball 90 miles per hour! Since then, he has kept pumping fastballs at an All-Star rate. Over the past 11 seasons, the Seattle Mariners' ace has become one of baseball's best, and most reliable. pitching superstars.

Felix grew up in Venezuela, a country that loves baseball. His father and uncle had both been baseball players. They taught him to pitch . . . fast! That 90-mile-per-hour fastball turned a lot of heads as Felix played on youth teams and all-star squads. The pro teams from the United States were watching carefully. As soon as Felix turned 16, he could sign with a big-league organization. The Seattle Mariners were the lucky winners after they offered him more than $700,000 to sign a contract! The teenager was a pro!

Felix spent two-plus seasons in the minors, learning the pro game as well as English. He was 30–10 with 363 strikeouts in a little more than 300 innings. The Mariners didn't wait. In the middle of the 2005 season, they brought up the 19-year-old star. Felix won 4 games that year, then improved to 12 wins in his second season. He continued to get better and better.

In 2009, he had his breakout year. "King Felix" earned his nickname by posting an American League-best 19 wins against only 5 losses. His ERA was an outstanding 2.49. He made his first All-Star team and was second in the voting for the Cy Young Award.

Voters in 2010 put him atop the Cy Young platform. Though his record was a modest 13–12, he led the AL with a 2.27 ERA while allowing the fewest hits per nine innings. There is more to being a great pitcher than just the "W" column!

Felix has become an established star. His fastball is still among the best in the majors, but he has become a smarter pitcher, too. He also learned the importance of staying in shape in the off-season, combining good diet and workouts. His hard work has paid off with a long, mostly injury-free career.

In 2014, Felix finished second in the Cy Young voting again. He won his second AL ERA title with a career-low 2.14 mark that year. He won 15 games that year, then added 18 wins in 2015.

The only thing he has not accomplished in his great career is pitching in the playoffs. But if the King has anything to say about it, that will change soon!

STAT BOX	W	ERA	IP	SO
2015	18	3.53	201.2	191
CAREER	143	3.11	2262.1	2142

BEFORE THE BIGS

After he signed with Seattle, but before he left for the United States, Felix got a chance to show off for the home folks. He spent the summer of 2002 playing in the Venezuelan League. Like many countries in and around the Caribbean, Venezuela has a popular pro league of its own.

FELIX HERNANDEZ

ERIC HOSMER
KANSAS CITY ROYALS

Position: FIRST BASE

Height: 6' 4"
Weight: 225 lbs

Throws: Left
Bats: Left

First MLB Season: 2011

At the heart of the Kansas City Royals' 2015 World Series championship team was a hardworking first baseman who had quietly become a team leader. Eric Hosmer came to the Royals as a first-round draft pick with high expectations. On and off the field, he has lived up to them . . . and more.

Eric grew up in Florida, where his father was a firefighter. Eric was a star player from his first days on the diamond. In youth baseball, he helped his teams win state championships. By high school, he was a left-handed slugger. As a senior, he hit 11 homers and batted .470. The Royals made him the number-three overall pick in the 2008 MLB Draft. Eric made his parents proud when he signed a $6 million deal to join the Royals organization.

As good as he was, Eric struggled a bit in his first pro seasons. He struck out too often and his power was way down. In 2010, doctors found that his eyesight was not as good as it could be. A minor surgery fixed the problem and—bingo!—the hits followed. Eric led his minor-league team to the Texas League title, hitting 6 homers in the playoffs.

Eric began the next year in the minors, too, but soon showed he was ready for the big leagues. He hit .439 over his first month in Triple-A, the top level of minor-league baseball. The Royals made him their starting first baseman in May 2011, and he's been in the Majors ever since.

Along with his great hitting skills (he has a .280 career average), Eric has become a top defensive first baseman. In 2013, he won the first of his three consecutive Gold Glove Awards.

Kansas City was slowly building a great team, keyed by Eric and other young stars such as Mike Moustakas, Alex Gordon, and Lorenzo Cain. In 2014, the Royals were the surprise AL wild-card team. The scrappy team made it all the way to the World Series, where it lost a heartbreaking Game 7 to the San Francisco Giants.

After the disappointment of 2014, the Royals came into 2015 with one goal: Win it all. Hosmer knew that he had to step up to keep the team going forward. He drove in a career-high 93 runs, while hitting 18 homers and batting an excellent .297.

In the postseason, Eric was amazing. In three series, he knocked in 17 runs. The Royals returned to the World Series, facing the New York Mets. Eric had the game-winning sacrifice fly in Kansas City's 5–4 victory in 14 innings in Game 1. He also scored a daring run in Game 5, racing home from third on a ground ball on the infield. His run tied the score in the ninth inning. The Royals went on to win the game and the Series in 12 innings, 7–2. Eric danced on the mound with his teammates in celebration, knowing they had made history.

The Royals certainly made the right choice back in 2008!

STAT BOX

	AVG	HR	RBI	OPS
2015	.297	18	93	.822
CAREER	.280	77	368	.763

BEFORE THE BIGS

To work on his swing, Eric spent hours in his backyard hitting baseballs into a net. It was a special net, though, with a ball attached to elastic cords. As soon as Eric smacked the ball, it bounced back into place, ready to hit again. He could swing and swing and never have to bend down to pick up the ball!

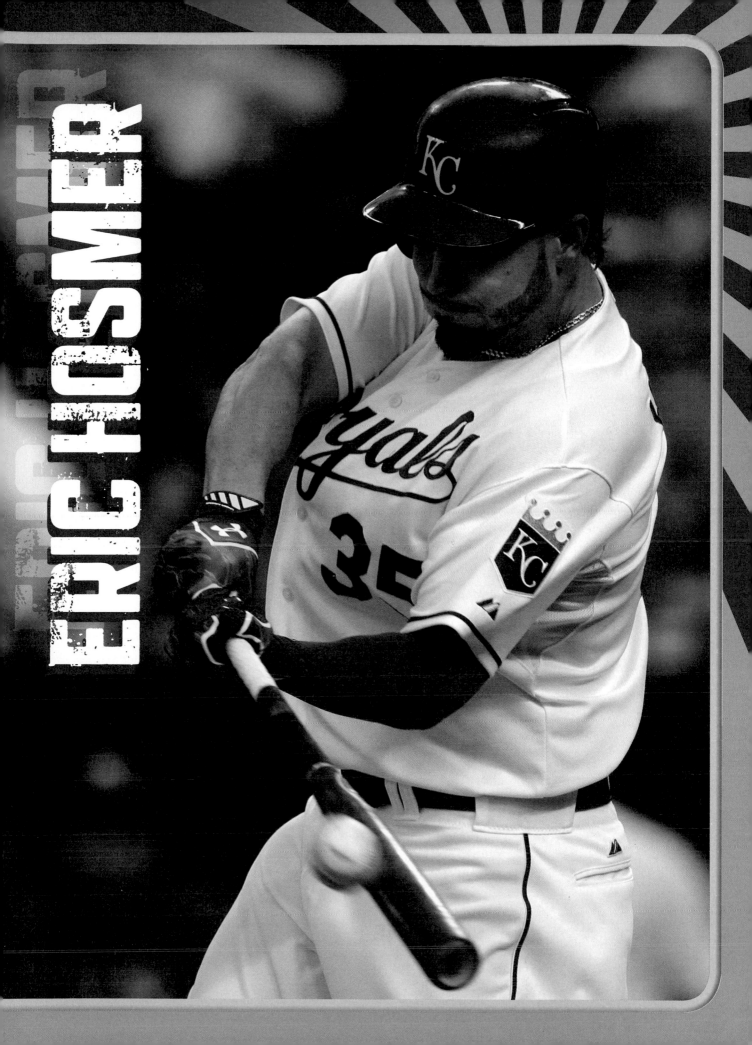

ERIC HOSMER

DALLAS KEUCHEL

HOUSTON ASTROS

Position: PITCHER

Height: 6'3"	Throws: Left
Weight: 210 lbs	Bats: Left

First MLB Season: 2012

Is it the beard? Has the marvelous mane on his chin made Dallas Keuchel (his last name is pronounced "KY-kull") one of baseball's best? Here's a secret: The Houston Astros pitcher didn't have a really big beard until the summer of 2014 . . . and that's when he blossomed into a star! Maybe the answer to being a great pitcher is to stop shaving!

Dallas did not grow up in Texas, as his name suggests. But he did grow up next door, in Oklahoma. His hometown is Tulsa, where he started playing baseball when he was about eight. After starring in youth leagues, he was a high school powerhouse. His school won the Oklahoma state championship when he was a sophomore and again when he was a senior. In his final year, he was 10–0 with a tiny 1.57 ERA.

Dallas moved on to the University of Arkansas. He was not a power pitcher there. His best skill was keeping the ball around the plate and not walking many batters. As a junior he helped the Razorbacks make the College World Series. He pitched and won 2 games in the Series. After that solid year, he was good enough for the Houston Astros to draft him in the seventh round.

Dallas' big-league career almost ended after a poor rookie season. He won his first game, but only two more after that. Heading into 2013, he wasn't even sure he would stay in the big leagues. But he did, and went on to make 22 starts and also some relief appearances.

In 2014, Dallas was a full-time starter. He posted his first winning record at 12–9 and led the American League with 5 complete games. His ERA dropped a lot, too, down to 2.93 (from 5.15 in 2013). Dallas was learning to combine his great command with a hard slider that kept hitters off balance. He also showed that he's more than just a thrower. He became the first Astros hurler ever to win the Gold Glove Award for fielding excellence.

The confidence Dallas earned in 2014 set him up for his breakout 2015 season. He started hot, winning seven of his first eight decisions. By July, he was 11–3! His first half was so great that he was named the American League's starting pitcher in the All-Star Game!

After that performance, he did even better in the second half. By the end of the season, he had won a career-high and AL-best 20 games, with an ERA of 2.48. The man with the famous beard was voted the AL Cy Young Award winner! He capped it off by winning 2 games in the postseason as the Astros made the playoffs for the first time since 2005.

STAT BOX	W	ERA	IP	SO
2015	20	2.48	232.0	216
CAREER	41	3.58	671.0	523

Dallas first learned about baseball by playing a handheld electronic game. He learned about hard work by mowing lawns in his neighborhood and by working at a store that sold honey-glazed ham!

DALLAS KEUCHEL

MANNY MACHADO

BALTIMORE ORIOLES

Position: THIRD BASE

Height: 6'3"
Weight: 185 lbs
Throws: Right
Bats: Right
First MLB Season: 2012

Manny Machado is one of the hottest young sluggers in baseball and one of the game's best fielders, too. So you would not expect the Baltimore Orioles third baseman to be overlooked. Still, he often is overshadowed by other young stars such as the Washington Nationals' Bryce Harper and the Los Angeles Angels' Mike Trout—which is just fine with him.

"I just go about my business, put up numbers, and do my thing," Machado says. "Just go out there, have fun, and everything else will fall in place." His baseball skills and his humble attitude have helped him do just that!

After Manny had a great high school career in Miami, the Orioles chose him with the third pick in the 2010 draft. To thank his mom for all the support she gave him—Manny's father was not around when he was a kid—he bought her a house with the big check he got for being drafted. Then Manny buzzed through the minors, crushing the best pitchers and playing amazing defense at third.

In 2012, the Orioles were in a pennant race and needed a boost. They called up Manny in early August, and he became that spark. He was only 19 years old but he had a pair of hits in his first game and 2 homers in his second! The Orioles won 33 of their last 51 regular-season games and made the playoffs.

In 2013, Manny became the team's regular third baseman and played in nearly every game. He led the American League in at-bats and doubles. He also won his first Gold Glove for defensive excellence. All of a league's Gold Glove winners also compete for a single award called the Platinum Glove as the top overall defender. At just 20 years old, Manny won that Platinum Glove!

Even though Manny arrived in the majors at a young age, he had plenty of big-league connections. He played with Harper on a national team in 2009. His best friend growing up was Yonder Alonso, who is now a first baseman for the Oakland Athletics (plus, Manny is married to Yonder's sister, Yainee!). And Alex Rodriguez, another former Miami high school standout (now with the New York Yankees), has been a mentor to the young star.

Those players and all his fans have watched Manny continue to get better. Though he missed part of 2014 with a knee injury, he came back strong in 2015. He made his second All-Star Game and won his second Gold Glove. He also slugged 35 homers and played in all 162 of the Orioles' games. He finished fourth in the balloting for the AL's Most Valuable Player award. There are a lot of baseball experts who expect this young all-around star to move up to first place in that voting in the years ahead.

STAT BOX

	AVG	HR	RBI	OPS
2015	.286	35	86	.861
CAREER	.281	68	215	.787

Manny's favorite team growing up was the Florida Marlins (now the Miami Marlins). Through his mom's job, he got tickets to games. He was in the stadium when the Marlins won the World Series in 2003!

MANNY MACHADO

ANDREW McCUTCHEN

PITTSBURGH PIRATES

Position: OUTFIELD

Height: 5'10"	**Throws:** Right
Weight: 200 lbs	**Bats:** Right

First MLB Season: 2009

Everyone in baseball can now see how special Andrew McCutchen is. The all-around star outfielder for the Pittsburgh Pirates has finished among the top five in the National League MVP voting every year since 2012. Plus, he has led his team back to a place among the game's best. But often lost in his story is this fact: In 2007, he went through a slump that he almost didn't escape.

Andrew started playing baseball as a youngster in Florida. He was a shortstop to begin with, the best athlete on every team he played for. He tore up the high school fields, batting above .700 as a senior. With 16 homers and 45 steals that year, he also showed the versatility that has made him great. The Pirates chose him with the 11th overall draft pick in 2005 and sent him to the minors. They knew their young player would be a star outfielder in the big leagues one day.

By 2007, however, the swing that helped him get drafted seemed to have disappeared. He was batting .189 in the worst slump of his career. Andrew worried that his pro career would burn out too quickly. So he sat down with coaches and broke down his swing. He made adjustments, worked in the batting cage, and slowly got things back on track. By the end of that season, he was hitting above .300. He kept up that pace for two more seasons.

Andrew joined the Pirates to stay in 2009 and became their everyday center fielder. With 22 steals and a .286 average, he was fourth in the NL Rookie of the Year voting. By 2011, he was an All-Star. In 2012, he led the NL with 194 hits. He won a Gold Glove Award for his fielding, and a Silver Slugger Award for his hitting.

That was nothing compared to 2013. That year, Andrew batted .317, knocked in 84 runs, and stole 27 bases. More importantly, he was the leader of a Pirates team that earned its first playoff spot since 1992! Andrew was voted as the NL MVP!

The Pirates have returned to the playoffs each season since, and Andrew has continued his all-around great play. He has been on the NL All-Star team each year since 2011.

In 2015, he also won the Roberto Clemente Award. It is named for a former Pirates great and given to a player who is an all-star on the field and in the community! Andrew runs "Cutch's Crew" to help inner-city kids in Pittsburgh. He also supports a number of other charities, including the Make-A-Wish Foundation and a children's hospital.

STAT BOX

2015	.292	23	96	.889
CAREER	.298	151	558	.884

BEFORE THE BIGS

When Andrew was in eighth grade, he was so good that he started at shortstop . . . for the high school varsity team! He hit above .500 for the season, too!

ANDREW McCUTCHEN

MIKE TROUT
LOS ANGELES ANGELS

Position: OUTFIELD

Height: 6'2"
Weight: 235 lbs

Throws: Right
Bats: Right

First MLB Season: 2011

On many baseball stats websites, league leaders are listed in **boldface** type. When you look at Mike Trout's five big-league seasons, there is a lot of **boldface** type! He has led the American League in **runs**, **stolen bases**, **RBI**, **slugging average**, and **total bases**! In every season from 2012 to 2015, he finished first or second in the AL MVP voting. **Wow!**

Mike started his road to greatness in a small town in New Jersey. He still returns there every off-season to see his parents and his many friends. For a player who has become the face of baseball, he remains humble and patient.

In high school, Mike first showed the amazing combination of speed and power that has made him a star. The Los Angeles Angels chose him with the 25th pick of the 2009 MLB Draft. (How mad are the 24 teams that passed Mike by!) After a quick visit to the minors, Mike was brought up to the big-league club in the summer of 2011.

Though Mike hit an amazing .342 in the minor leagues, he struggled at first with the Angels. It was an adjustment to face Major League pitching. Mike felt a lot of pressure, too, as the "future" of the Angels. He hit only .220 and stole only 4 bases in 40 games.

In 2012, however, he was really ready. He dazzled fans and opponents with his speed, leading the AL with 49 steals and 129 runs. His .326 average was second in the league. In the newer category of WAR (Wins Above Replacement), he was the best in the game! Mike was voted as the AL Rookie of the Year and finished second in the MVP voting.

Mike had set a high bar for excellence . . . and has lived up to it and more! He had his finest season in 2014, when he led the AL in runs, RBI, and total bases. He was named the league's MVP. At 23 years old, he was the youngest player ever to get every first-place vote in the balloting. He also was the MVP of that summer's All-Star Game!

In 2015, Mike's stolen bases dropped to 11, but he turned on the power. He blasted a career-best 41 home runs and led the league with a .590 slugging percentage.

Along with his offensive skills, Mike is a dynamic defender. He has climbed outfield walls to rob several players of home runs, and base runners rarely challenge his arm.

When listing baseball's best all-around players, put Mike's name at the top of the list . . . in **boldface** type!

STAT BOX	AVG	HR	RBI	OPS
2015	.299	41	90	.991
CAREER	.304	139	397	.956

BEFORE THE BIGS

How much of an all-around star was Mike in high school?

He played pitcher along with being an outfielder. In one game, he threw a no-hitter while striking out 18 batters! He was such a great hitter that an opponent once walked Mike intentionally . . . with the bases loaded!

MIKE TROUT

HERE'S A QUICK LOOK AT THE TOP ROOKIES FROM 2015. WATCH FOR THEM IN ALL-STAR GAMES IN THE YEARS TO COME!

KRIS BRYANT

THIRD BASE • CHICAGO CUBS

All the writers agreed. When the votes were in for National League Rookie of the Year, Kris Bryant was the unanimous choice. He had slugged 26 homers, drove in 99 runs, and helped the Cubs make the playoffs. After being drafted number two overall in 2013, Bryant was in the spotlight from his first game, and he responded with power!

CARLOS CORREA

SHORTSTOP • HOUSTON ASTROS

As Houston roared to the playoffs, Carlos played a key role. The 20-year-old native of Puerto Rico (he turned 21 late in the season) slugged 22 homers in only 99 games and played a graceful shortstop. He was named the American League Rookie of the Year. As the youngest non-pitcher in the Majors, Carlos looks like he'll have many years of greatness ahead of him!

ROOKIES

FRANCISCO LINDOR
SHORTSTOP • CLEVELAND INDIANS

Close behind Carlos in the AL Rookie of the Year race was this Cleveland infielder. Francisco Lindor not only became one of the best fielding shortstops in baseball, he also batted .313 in 2015. Also from Puerto Rico, Francisco was only 21 last season. He figures to anchor Cleveland's infield for many years.

LUIS SEVERINO
PITCHER • NEW YORK YANKEES

The New York Yankees needed pitching help and called Luis up in August. Pitching in Yankee Stadium is always packed with pressure. But as the team battled for the playoffs, Luis did his part, winning five of his seven decisions in September. He showed off a great fastball and big-game calm. Now when Luis pitches, the pressure is on the batters!

2015 MLB
FINAL STANDINGS

AMERICAN LEAGUE

EAST

Toronto Blue Jays	93–69
New York Yankees	87–75
Baltimore Orioles	81–81
Tampa Bay Rays	80–82
Boston Red Sox	78–84

CENTRAL

Kansas City Royals	95–67
Minnesota Twins	83–79
Cleveland Indians	81–80
Chicago White Sox	76–86
Detroit Tigers	74–87

WEST

Texas Rangers	88–74
Houston Astros	86–76
Los Angeles Angels	85–77
Seattle Mariners	76–86
Oakland Athletics	68–94

NATIONAL LEAGUE

EAST

New York Mets	90–72
Washington Nationals	83–79
Miami Marlins	71–91
Atlanta Braves	67–95
Philadelphia Phillies	63–99

CENTRAL

St. Louis Cardinals	100–62
Pittsburgh Pirates	98–64
Chicago Cubs	97–65
Milwaukee Brewers	68–94
Cincinnati Reds	64–98

WEST

Los Angeles Dodgers	92–70
San Francisco Giants	84–78
Arizona Diamondbacks	79–83
San Diego Padres	74–88
Colorado Rockies	68–94